Barn Bear's big scare

Liz Lewis

Geographical Association

In Edinburgh city, Barnaby's class,
are doing their fieldwork with Mrs Glass.

They see a big rock. It is high and steep.
And right at the top is the castle keep.

Mrs Glass asks why they think it was right, for the castle to be built high up on this site?

'I'll show you all if you come to this side,'
Why the rock is so steep.' says Andy, the guide.

On the display boards is information, about the castle rock's formation.

It shows a volcano and lava flowing, and molten magma, red and glowing

'Now this is the end of our lesson on rock.'
Andy smiles to himself as he looks at the clock.

There's a terrible bang! The castle walls quake... and Barnaby's paws begin to shake.

'An eruption!' he cries, 'An attack on the keep!'
He falls to the floor in a terrified heap.

Mrs Glass and the class think it's fantastic fun,
to see Barnaby scared of the one o'clock gun!